Mountain Lion

Published in the United States of America by Cherry Lake Publishing
Ann Arbor, Michigan
www.cherrylakepublishing.com

Reading Adviser: Marla Conn MS, Ed., Literacy specialist, Read-Ability, Inc.
Book Design: Jennifer Wahi
Illustrator: Jeff Bane

Photo Credits: © Warren Metcalf / Shutterstock.com, 5; © Suha Derbent / Shutterstock.com, 7, 19; © Brian Millenbach / Shutterstock.com, 9; © Joseph Sohm / Shutterstock.com, 11; © Jack Nevitt / Shutterstock.com, 13; © Geoffrey Kuchera / Shutterstock.com, 15; © Michal Ninger / Shutterstock.com, 17; © Baranov E / Shutterstock.com, 21; © iva / Shutterstock.com, 23; © Ozerina Anna 2-3, 24; Cover, 1, 8, 12, 20, Jeff Bane

Library of Congress Cataloging-in-Publication Data has been filed and is available at catalog.loc.gov

Printed in the United States of America
Corporate Graphics

table of contents

About the author: Dr. Virginia Loh-Hagan is an author, university professor, former classroom teacher, and curriculum designer. She's seen mountain lions while walking her dogs. She lives in San Diego with her very tall husband and very naughty dogs. To learn more about her, visit www.virginialoh.com.

About the illustrator: Jeff Bane and his two business partners own a studio along the American River in Folsom, California, home of the 1849 Gold Rush. When Jeff's not sketching or illustrating for clients, he's either swimming or kayaking in the river to relax.

Mountain lions are tan. They have a white face. They have a white belly. They're also called pumas or cougars.

Mountain lions weigh up to 130 pounds (59 kilograms). They are 2 feet (61 centimeters) tall. They have big paws with sharp claws. Mountain lions are thin.

They have strong legs. They can jump high. They jump far.

Mountain lions live in the United States. They live in Canada. Some live in South America.

What do you do in bad weather?

Mountain lions live all over. They like mountains and woods. They like deserts. They like **swamps**. They find caves for **shelter**.

food

Mountain lions only eat meat. They hunt at night. They eat deer. They eat mice. They eat any animals they catch.

Mountain lions are good hunters. They follow **prey**. They catch it. They kill. They drag prey away. They hide it. They eat over a few days.

Mountain lions have special backbones. They bend easily. This helps them run and jump. This helps them climb and swim.

They like to be alone. They are shy. They guard their space.

Baby mountain lions are **kittens**. They are born with spots. Their spots fade at 6 months.

glossary

kittens (KIT-uhnz) baby mountain lions

prey (PRAY) animals that are hunted for food

shelter (SHEL-tur) a place that keeps an animal safe from bad weather or danger

swamps (SWAHMPS) areas of soft, wet ground

index